MARY LOU
RETTON

MARY LOU RETTON

A Biography by
GEORGE SULLIVAN

JULIAN MESSNER
New York

PHOTO CREDITS: AP/Wide World, title page, pgs. 6, 18, 20, 21, 30, 37, 52, 53, 54, 77; George Sullivan, pgs. 13, 66, 69, 73; Michele Plutro, pgs. 16, 28, 35, 44, 75; Fairmont *Times-West Virginian,* pgs. 25, 32, 64; Holland Wemple, pg. 62.

Published by JULIAN MESSNER
A Division of Simon & Schuster, Inc.
Simon & Schuster Building
1230 Avenue of the Americas
New York, New York 10020
Also Available in Wanderer Trade Edition.
Designed by Stanley S. Drate/Folio Graphics Co., Inc.
Manufactured in the United States of America
10 9 8 7 6 5 4 3 2
JULIAN MESSNER and colophon are trademarks
of Simon & Schuster, Inc.
Library of Congress Cataloging in Publication Data
Sullivan, George, 1927-
    Mary Lou Retton.
    Summary: A biography of the sixteen-year-old athlete
whose performance at the 1984 Olympics made her the first
American woman to win a gold medal in gymnastics.
    1. Retton, Mary Lou, 1968-   —Juvenile literature.
2. Gymnasts—United States—Biography—Juvenile literature.
[1. Retton, Mary Lou, 1968-   . 2. Gymnasts]
I. Title.
GV460.2.R47S84   1985   796.4'1'0924 [B] [92]   84-25717
ISBN 0-671-55473-5 (lib. bdg.)
ISBN 0-671-55472-7 (pbk.)

Contents

Mary Lou Retton jumps for joy as her perfect "10" flashes across scoreboard at the 1984 Olympics.

1 ★☆☆

GOLDEN GIRL

It came down to the final event. For almost a week, 16-year-old Mary Lou Retton, America's best female gymnast, had sparred with Romania's Ecaterina Szabo for the gold medal in all-around gymnastics in the 1984 Olympic Games in Los Angeles. The winner would bear the title of finest woman gymnast in the world.

The competition had been nip and tuck. Then Szabo, a solid international star who rarely made a mistake, twirled around the uneven bars with her usual brilliance, earning a score of 9.90.

Now it was Mary Lou's turn on the vault, the last chance for the 4-foot 9-inch, 92-pound dynamo to take home the gold.

As Mary Lou waited her turn, her personal coach, Bela Karolyi, leaned across the barricade that separated him from the contestants and handed her a piece of paper. On it he had done some arithmetic: "Score a 9.95 and you will tie Szabo for the gold. Score a perfect 10 and you will be the all-around champion. Anything less than 9.95 means second place."

In the long history of the Olympics, no American woman had ever won an individual medal of any kind in gymnastics competition. A team bronze in 1948 had been the best American achievement. Winning an individual *gold* medal seemed out of the question.

Karolyi reached down and shook Mary Lou's shoulders. She nodded intensely.

Mary Lou stood at the end of the runway. She smoothed out imaginary wrinkles in her stars-and-stripes uniform, then chalked her hands and rubbed them together. She shook her hair and tossed her head back.

At last the green light over the scoreboard came on signaling that it was her turn. A tense silence came over the thousands of spectators in Pauley Pavilion.

Mary Lou's powerful legs sent her roaring down the seventy-five feet of runway. She leaped onto the springboard then pushed her handspring high toward the rafters. She twisted and turned and then "stuck it"—landed on the dark blue mat without having to move so much as a toe—and thrust her hands high above her head.

As the crowd roared its approval, Mary Lou ran to the barricade to hug Karolyi. Then she hopped back onto the runway to wave to the crowd and shake her fists over her head.

"10! . . . 10! . . . 10!" screamed the spectators. "10! . . . 10! . . . 10!"

Moments later the 10 flashed on the electronic scoreboard. Mary Lou Retton had done it.

That one dramatic moment changed Mary Lou's life forever. Becoming an Olympic champion was only part of it. She became, said the *New York Times*, an "American folk heroine."

It wasn't simply that Mary Lou happened to be superskilled, performing routines that somehow seemed magical in their complexity. It was her personality too. When she heard that her dramatic vault had earned a 10, Mary Lou was aglow, bouncing up and down and flashing a smile big enough to light up living rooms all across America.

Mail arrived by the sackful at the Retton home on Beverly Road in Fairmont, West Virginia. The telephone never stopped ringing. Mary Lou could not set foot outside her door without being recognized. People constantly besieged her for autographs and snapshots.

She became a cover girl for *Sports Illustrated*, *Newsweek*, and many other magazines. Her hometown had a parade in her honor and named a street after her. She signed big endorsement contracts with major advertisers.

"Well, nobody thought it could be done," Mary Lou said afterward. "But you know what, I went and did it."

But doing it had not been easy.

It meant leading a strictly disciplined life. There were plenty of times she longed for a candy bar or a slice of pizza, yet had to restrain herself.

It meant leaving her parents, relatives, and friends and moving to a strange city; it meant being homesick.

It meant putting her social life on hold for half of her teenage years.

It meant pain and injury—a broken wrist, torn knee cartilage, and so many bumps and bruises that her mother once borrowed a high-impact flak jacket from the local high school football team for her to wear.

Was it worth it? Ask Mary Lou that question and she answers with a winning smile.

Many people have dreams, but only a few live them. Mary Lou Retton is one.

2

☆☆
☆

FAIRMONT

Fairmont, West Virginia, is a medium-size Ohio Valley coal mining and industrial town on the banks of the Monongahela River in northern West Virginia about ninety miles south of Pittsburgh. Before Mary Lou Retton, its principal claim to fame was that it was the first city in the United States where Father's Day was celebrated.

It is the kind of town where yellow school buses clog early morning traffic and people don't hesitate to say "Good Morning" to a stranger.

Fairmont has always been a sportsminded community. The people cheer for the basketball and football teams of Fairmont State and West Virginia University in nearby Morgantown. High school sports are important too.

But in the months following her medal blitz at the Olympic Games, the Fairmont Falcons and West Virginia's Mountaineers were often overshadowed by Mary Lou. Fairmont and the surrounding area became Mary Lou Retton country.

Visitors to Fairmont couldn't help but become aware of what had happened. Approaching Fairmont, a sign alongside Interstate 79 declared: Marion County, Home of Mary Lou Retton, Olympic Gold Medalist. A white banner with gold lettering over a downtown street said simply: Fairmont—Mary Lou Retton.

Mary Lou Retton was born in Fairmont on January 24, 1968, to Lois and Ronnie Retton, who were both from large Italian families. The family name had been Rotunda when Mary Lou's greatgrandfather came to America from Italy many years before. Mary Lou was the youngest in a family of three boys and two girls.

The family was very sportsminded. Mary Lou's father, though only 5-foot 7-inches tall, was a guard and cocaptain for the West Virginia Mountaineers during the team's glory years in the late 1950s. The team, which starred Jerry West, one of basketball's all-time greats, got as far as the NCAA (National Collegiate Athletic Association) final matchup in 1959, only to be beaten, 71–70, by the University of California.

Mary Lou's father also played shortstop for a farm team of the New York Yankees in Richmond, Virginia. At the time, the Yankees boasted such Hall of Famers as Mickey Mantle and Roger Maris, which is one reason why Mr. Retton never made it to the big leagues. He was a .270 hitter.

There was always sports equipment around the Retton home and the children became naturally involved; the three boys in baseball, and the girls in dance, acrobatics and gymnastics.

Like her brothers and sister, Mary Lou walked early—at nine months. And she walked well, without falling or stumbling.

She was a very active child. Mrs. Retton has said that she thinks her daughter's toughness came from being the baby in a big family—she got her muscular legs from running errands for everybody, according to Mrs. Retton. "Go get me this," or, "Run upstairs and do that," were words young Mary Lou often heard. "Her brothers picked on her and wrestled with her. It made her tough."

When she was four, her parents enrolled Mary Lou and her sister Shari, then nine, in a dance class at a local gym. Two evenings each week they were taught the basics of ballet, tap, jazz and acrobatics.

The dance program was headed by Linda Burdette, the gymnastics coach at the University of West Virginia. Burdette was impressed by the Retton sisters and spent extra time working with them.

"They learned so fast!" she once told the Fairmont *Times–West Virginian*. "It was incredible what they could do after such a short period of time.

"They had an awareness, an air sense that is unbelievable for girls at that level. Like a cat, they would never fall on their heads or back; they always landed on their hands or feet."

Mary Lou first entertained audiences when she was nine or ten. Thousands of residents of northern West Virginia and southwestern Pennsylvania remember her and her sister as among the young halftime entertainers at West Virginia basketball games. As part of their routine, they performed continuous back handsprings topped off with back somersaults. "They always had the crowd on their feet," Burdette recalls.

Her mother remembers Mary Lou as being a very happy and funloving child. Besides dancing and acrobatics, she liked swimming and listening to music. She collected stuffed lambs. She was a familiar figure at her brother's baseball games, always accompanied by her big collie named Tarzan.

Where food was concerned, her favorite dishes were Italian, especially manicotti—large noodles stuffed with a soft cheese and baked in tomato sauce.

In the Retton's big, stately brick home on Beverly Road in the hilly Watson section of Fairmont, Mary Lou shared

The Retton home in Fairmont, West Virginia.

a bedroom with Shari. It was home to her collection of stuffed lambs, one tattered member of which served Mary Lou as a good luck charm.

Much of what was later displayed in the room represented Mary Lou's gymnastics career—medals and trophies and one wall covered with ribbons, most of them blue.

Mr. and Mrs. Retton wanted to find out how Mary Lou and Shari would respond to gymnastics training and enrolled them at the Aerial-Port Gymnastics Center in Fairmont. There they were coached by Gary Rafaloski, college teammate of onetime U.S. Olympic gymnast Kurt Thomas. Under Rafaloski, Mary Lou quickly moved from a Class Three to a Class One gymnast.

The lives of Mary Lou and Shari began to take separate paths at that time. Shari had entered high school and had become involved in many new activities, including preparing for college. Mary Lou was still in grade school at St. Anthony's, just down the road from the Retton home, and was young enough to compete in local and state meets.

Shari's gymnastics skill eventually earned her a scholarship to the University of West Virginia. As a freshman, she won All-American honors in four events, becoming the first woman at West Virginia to do so.

"I really started too late to have any notion of becoming an Olympic prospect," Shari has said. "There's a definite advantage to starting at an early age." One of Shari's ambitions was to become a gymnastics coach.

As Shari and Mary Lou were beginning to become known on the local gymnastics scene, their brothers were also starting to make names for themselves. Younger brother Jerry became an outstanding baseball, basketball and football player at West Fairmont High School. Donnie, the middle brother, became a catcher on Fairmont State's baseball team, while Ronnie played baseball at West Virginia University. To help their hitting, the Retton brothers had their own batting cage in the backyard.

Mary Lou was still in training at the Aerial-Port Gymnastic Center in 1982 when she first gave a hint of what was to come by sweeping the all-around title and every individual event at the South African Cup competition in Capetown, South Africa.

Perhaps it was then that Rafaloski, a gentle, quiet man, realized that he was eventually going to have to give up his star pupil. Mary Lou had simply outgrown Aerial-Port.

Rafaloski was beginning to evaluate other schools for her when Mary Lou made the move herself. At first, Rafaloski expressed some bitterness. "I was hurt," he once told United Press International. "I think any other coach in my shoes would be."

Rafaloski continued to coach young gymnasts at Aerial-Port. He served as an official at the Olympic Games in Los Angeles in 1984 where he was, as one might imagine, one of Mary Lou's most enthusiastic supporters.

3 ★☆ ☆

AMERICAN ORIGINAL

At first there was Ludmila Turischeva—tall, willowy, and graceful. She won the all-around gymnastics title for the Soviet Union in the 1972 Munich Olympic Games.

Also in 1972, also for the Soviets, came Olga Korbut—cute, pixieish, with yarn-tied pigtails. Olga picked up golds in free exercise and on the balance beam.

In 1976 at Montreal the star was Nadia Comaneci, all-around titlist, gold medal winner on the balance beam and bars, and the first Olympian to earn a perfect score in gymnastics competition.

Mary Lou, who was eight years old at the time, remembers stretching out on the floor of the family room at home and watching Nadia. "I was just a beginner," she has said. "I never thought about the gold medal. I just thought Nadia was great."

Nadia was elegant, but remote. A "butterfly," her coach Bela Karolyi called her. With routines characterized by grace and finesse, a television commentator described Nadia as "swimming in an ocean of air."

From the very beginning, it was obvious that Mary Lou was not going to be another Nadia Comaneci or Olga

Mary Lou during Olympic trials. Her "boxy torso" and "heavily muscled thighs" distinguished her from other lithe-looking gymnasts.

Korbut. Pixieish dancing didn't fit Mary Lou. Cuteness was out. Mary Lou was a gymnast with a difference, an American original.

Her boxy torso and heavily muscled thighs made Mary Lou a kind of gymnast people weren't used to seeing. Although short enough, she wasn't light and agile looking. "Ponytailed and real skinny, that's how everybody pictures a gymnast," Mary Lou observed. "But that's not me. I'm stocky and short."

Power was what Mary Lou was all about. No other gymnast could generate her speed or leap to her heights.

"Mary Lou has two great qualities that put her where she is," Don Peters, coach of the U.S. women's gymnastics team, once said. "First, physically she is the most powerful gymnast who ever competed in the sport, and she takes advantage of that in tumbling and vaulting.

"Second, she is one hell of a competitor. As the pressure gets greater, she gets greater."

In time, Mary Lou would change the nature of gymnastics in America, triggering a new trend which emphasizes highly difficult and very athletic stunts.

The vault was Mary Lou's best event. Vaulting begins with a sprint down a 75-foot mat toward a stationary leather horse (a padded piece of equipment about 5 feet long and a foot wide, standing 3½ feet above the floor). An instant before the gymnast reaches the horse, she pounds down on a springboard to help propel her into the air. She lands with her hands on the horse, then thrusts herself into the air for twists, turns and somersaults, then dismounts to land on her feet, legs together, arms up and back.

The run before the takeoff is usually a tip-off on how good the vault is going to be. "The faster you run, the higher you're going to go," says Mary Lou. "You want to go high and far and *stick* a landing. You don't want to land and do ten million steps; you want to land and just stay there."

Mary Lou also excelled in floor exercise. "Mary Lou is a little volcano on the floor," her coach once said of her.

In floor exercise, performed on a 40-foot-square mat, each gymnast has from one to one-and-a-half minutes to demonstrate her special talents in a carefully choreographed routine consisting of three tumbling pieces connected by dance movements such as leaps, turns, and pirouettes. It is the only gymnastics event performed to music.

Speaking of her style in floor exercise, Mary Lou once

Vaulting was Mary Lou's best event.

said: "I couldn't go out doing a floor routine ballet-style or something like that. I have to have strong and powerful music and do a lot of leaps and jumps." Mary Lou's routine included an extremely difficult tumbling move: a double back layout somersault with a full twist.

Floor exercise was one of Mary Lou's favorite events. Not only could she exert herself, but the event enabled her to be an actress. "You can play to everybody," she said. "You can show off a little. That's natural for me."

The balance beam is similar to floor exercise in that it features a combination of tumbling movements—cartwheels, handsprings, and somersaults—and dance elements including turns, jumps, leaps, and pirouettes.

The beam is four feet above the floor, sixteen feet long, and only four inches wide. It's something like a tightrope without a net. A short lapse in concentration or a move that is less than exact will result in a tumble. "It's just so hard to stay on that little piece of wood," says Mary Lou.

The young gymnast has never been crazy about the balance beam. In the other events, the bars, vault, and floor exercise, Mary Lou could "unload" or go all out. She couldn't unload on the balance beam but had to stay in control and concentrate.

Gymnasts have different methods of mounting the beam. Some simply step onto it, while others use a tumbling move such as a front or back somersault, back handspring, or a combination of these.

At the end of her routine, each gymnast performs a dramatic dismount. Mary Lou's dismount is especially difficult: a double back somersault, sometimes combined with a full twist.

As in floor exercise, the beam requires gymnasts to be good actresses. "Even if I fall, I have to pretend I'm out there enjoying myself. I try to smile," Mary Lou once said.

Whereas the beam and floor exercise emphasize grace

The Olympic Wondergirl performs on the balance beam.

and rhythm, the uneven bars require exceptional upper body strength. (The bars are actually fiberglass rods, and are called uneven because they are placed at different distances from the floor. The lower bar is at most 4-feet 11-inches from the floor; the upper, $7^1/_2$ feet.)

Each gymnast, hands on the bars, circles them, and supports herself from them, all in a carefully worked out routine.

Mary Lou developed a routine on the bars that has been named after her, an honor accorded no other female gymnast.

Called the Retton Salto, it begins with a giant swing into a handstand on the high bar, followed by a swoop down to a bellybeat on the low bar, performed with a

Mary Lou's performance on the uneven bars resulted in having a routine named after her— The Retton Salto.

resounding *Blam!* against the bar. She then swings up, lets go and does a front somersault in the pike position and lands sitting on the high bar again.

While Mary Lou favored the vault and floor exercise, she was often unbeatable in all four events. Her secret? "It's got to be natural," she once said, meaning that you have to work so hard, drilling yourself day after day, going over everything again and again, that even the most complex moves become as natural as brushing your hair or riding a bicycle. Said Mary Lou: "You should be able to do your entire routine in your pajamas. Without one mistake."

Gymnasts don't compete against one another the way runners or tennis players do. Each gymnast performs for a panel of judges who evaluates the performance of the routine.

A perfect score in any event is 10.00. Women gymnasts begin their routines with a score of 9.50 and men start at 9.40.

During the performance, judges deduct points for mistakes and award points for originality and difficulty of the routine. Such factors as the gymnast's style and even attire can also have a bearing on the scoring.

At major competitions, there are four judges plus one head judge assigned to each piece of apparatus. Each of the four judges independently arrives at a score and gives the mark to the head judge who then throws out the high and low scores and averages the two in the middle.

The head judge also scores the routine. If he or she feels the scores of the other judges do not accurately reflect the gymnast's performance, a conference is called and the score is reevaluated. In such cases, the head judge has the final word.

Anyone familiar with international gymnastics competition knows that politics can affect scoring. In other words, a judge's national allegiance can play a role in the awarding of points or in his or her refusal to award them.

Thus, controversy is possible over the way in which routines are judged. By lowering the score of one gymnast, even slightly, it's possible for a judge to help another gymnast win.

"Team gold medals have been won by tenths of a point," American gymnast Kathy Johnson once pointed out. "All those tenths of a point add up."

Gymnastic scoring can cause frustration among the performers. What one earns may not be what one gets from the judges.

4 ★ ☆ ☆

ON THE WAY

During 1982, while still being coached by Gary Rafaloski in Fairmont, Mary Lou traveled with him and her parents to win the ESPN (Entertainment and Sports Programming Network) single elimination competition in Las Vegas.

There the Rettons met Bela Karolyi who was before long to become the most important man in Mary Lou's life.

Karolyi had long been hailed as the best gymnastics coach in the world. In his native Romania, Karolyi and his wife, Marta, had produced many world championship women's teams as well as individual stars. Romanian women coached by the Karolyis had won ten world titles and five Olympic titles during the 1970s. The most noted of Karolyi's champions, Nadia Comaneci, captured three gold medals at the 1976 Olympics in Montreal and earned an unprecedented seven perfect scores of 10. Nadia then went on to earn one gold and three silvers at the 1980 Moscow Olympics.

After Nadia won worldwide fame, the Romanian government began to exercise more and more control over the Karolyi's gymnastics school, making them feel stifled by the interference.

In March 1981, Karolyi and his wife traveled to the United States with the Romanian team for a gymnastics meet in New York City. During the trip the Karolyis came to a decision: they would not return to their homeland; they would defect and adopt the United States as their country.

It was a wrenching decision. Their 11-year-old daughter was back in Romania and they spoke little English.

On the morning the Romanian team was to leave, Karolyi gathered the team together and explained his decision. The girls cried along with Karolyi.

From that day on the Karolyis began creating new lives for themselves. They first accepted jobs as gymnastics coaches at the University of Oklahoma, but later moved to Houston, Texas. In Houston, Karolyi began building an empire. He operated Karolyi Gymnastics, a huge, modern training center with several hundred students. Sprinkled among them were several of the nation's highest ranked women. A sign outside the building said: U.S. Gymnastics Center.

Karolyi and his wife were always on the scene, Karolyi directing the athletes, barking commands. He once told United Press International: "People said the American kids did not work hard enough and were not dedicated enough and were not serious enough about their work. But that's just not true.

Coach Bela Karolyi

"The kids are the same all over. If they are guided in the right way, they can be motivated."

Not only was Mary Lou impressed with Karolyi himself when she met him in Las Vegas, but she was also impressed by his gymnasts, by how thoroughly they had been prepared, and by their confidence. She began begging her parents to let her go to Houston to train with Karolyi. She believed that under his guidance she could become one of the best gymnasts in the world.

Her parents refused to let her go, saying she was too young. But Mary Lou persisted. After meets, she would come home crying, "But Mom, I could be the best!"

Finally her parents yielded. Not only were they influenced by Mary Lou herself, but they realized that she had already peaked in Fairmont. There were other mountains for her to climb. *"We've got to give her this chance,"* her father thought. *"If we don't it's something we might regret for the rest of our lives."*

Late in 1982, Mary Lou left home for Houston and Bela Karolyi. It was Christmastime when she said her goodbyes. Leaving home was very hard.

It was arranged that Mary Lou would live with the Spiller family in Houston. Paige Spiller, 15, was also a student at Karolyi's school.

Paige had two brothers, 20-year-old Preston, and Patrick who was 9. Said Mary Lou: "They punch me and pick on me just like my own brothers."

It was not easy for Mary Lou at first. She admitted she got a little "weepy" sometimes. Her mother kept her up-to-date on family news by writing to her every day.

Enrolling at Karolyi's school meant plenty of hard work. She trained at the gym twice every day. She would train in the morning, then go home and have lunch. She would watch "The Guiding Light" on television, then it was back to the gym to train from 6:00 to 9:00. She would return home for dinner and then go to sleep.

That was her life. The rigid routine left little time for studying. She dropped out of high school and began taking correspondence courses which permitted her to study at a slower pace.

She didn't go to dances or football games. "Boys," she said, "have to wait."

Holidays? They were very rare. One year, for example, Karolyi switched Christmas to October. That's when he gave his students their holiday break. All of the important gymnastics meets are held in December. "There was no way we could go home then," explained Mary Lou.

In some ways, though Mary Lou managed to remain a typical teenager. She swooned over actor Matt Dillon and loved cruising shopping malls on Saturday afternoons. She dreamed of getting a Porsche once she had her driver's license.

Of all the gymnasts at Karolyi's school at the time, the most prized was Dianne Durham, 14, from Gary, Indiana. Dianne had speed and strength, dedication and confidence. She also had the distinction of being ranked the No. 1 female gymnast in the United States.

Dianne, who began her gymnastics training as a 4-year-old, had gotten homesick in Houston, so her mother had moved there temporarily. To become an Olympic champion was Dianne's goal. If she could realize that ambition, she would become the first black ever to win an Olympic medal in the sport.

Dianne and Mary Lou became good friends, but were also rivals. Mary Lou always felt that whatever Dianne could do, she could do too.

When Karolyi coached Nadia Comaneci he was tough. He talked in a gruff voice. His face seldom wore anything but a scowl.

Mary Lou with Dianne Durham.

But once settled in America, Karolyi thawed out. He became an enthusiastic cheerleader, constantly shouting words of encouragement during competitions, clapping his gymnasts on the back, and rewarding displays of excellence with big bear hugs.

Mary Lou responded well to this type of treatment. It psyched her up.

The positive influence that Karolyi had upon Mary Lou was first demonstrated at an invitational meet held at Caesar's Palace in Las Vegas early in 1983, only a week or so after Mary Lou's fifteenth birthday. Besides Mary Lou, Karolyi brought Dianne Durham to the meet.

Two very well known gymnasts were entered in the event: Tracee Talavera and Julianne McNamara. Both had trained at the National Academy in Eugene, Oregon, under Dick Mulvihill, one of the most respected of all coaches. Within the past year, however, Julianne had left Mulvihill to train with Don Peters of the Southern

· California Acro-Team, or SCAT. (Later Julianne would switch from Peters to Karolyi in Houston.)

A native of Flushing, Queens, in New York, whose family had moved to California, Julianne had been competing nationally and internationally for almost five years. In that time she had come to rank as one of the country's most skilled gymnasts, if not *the* most. Ponytailed and blonde, she stood 4-foot 10^1/$_2$-inches tall and weighed 84 pounds.

Julianne was the American national champion in 1980. She placed seventh in the all-around competition in the 1981 World Championships in Moscow, which was the highest all-around ranking ever achieved in world championship competition. At the time, Julie was America's best hope for a gold medal in the 1984 Olympic Games.

At the Caesar's Palace Invitational, Julianne and Tracee Talavera both had problems. Julianne won the uneven bars competition with a 1.90, but in the floor exercise she took a couple of spills that kept her out of contention for the all-around title. Tracee became the beam titlist, with a score of 9.85, but also had difficulties in the floor exercise.

It was Mary Lou who won the all-around title. She hit everything. One of her best moments came during the floor exercise. Executing a double back layout, her arms at her sides, her legs fully extended, she looked like a metal rod twisting through the air.

For her efforts, Mary Lou was awarded a trophy nearly as tall as herself. In an interview afterward, she was asked by a television broadcaster how it felt to outdo big-name competitors like Julianne and Tracee.

Mary Lou didn't hold back. "It feels *great*," she said, "and this is my first time, you know, beating top seniors, and it feels absolutely excellent."

She also realized how her victory might affect her standing within the gymnastics community. "Name rec-

Mary Lou performs on the balance beam at McDonald's American Cup competition.

ognition is very important in gymnastics," she said. "I hope this boosts me right up there."

A month later, Mary Lou again astounded the gymnastics world with her performance in the McDonald's American Cup Competition held at New York's Madison Square Garden.

At the time, Mary Lou wasn't ranked high enough to earn an invitation to the meet. When she and her teammates from Karolyi's school arrived for the competition, Mary Lou was merely a "sub"—a benchwarmer. But just before the meet got underway, Dianne Durham suffered a hip injury and Mary Lou was called upon to fill in.

The field consisted of forty-four gymnasts from fourteen countries, including Romania, Japan, the Soviet Union and Germany. In previous years, the European countries had used the American Cup competition to showcase some of their younger, up-and-coming athletes. But in 1983, instead of displaying young hopefuls, the various countries had brought their top stars. "The Olympics are next year," said Don Peters, Julianne McNamara's coach at the time, "and I think everybody wants to establish themselves."

Mary Lou was a sensation. Not only did she win the competition, but she set a meet record of 9.95 points in the vault event. She finished with 39.30 points for the four events. Julianne McNamara, who had been the American Cup winner in 1981 and 1982, finished second with 39.00 points.

One thing that amazed observers was that Julianne posted a higher score in finishing second than she had been able to reach in either of her winning years, yet Mary Lou still beat her. In other words, Mary Lou had raised the competition to a higher level.

"It finally made me feel that all the hard work is worthwhile," a glowing Mary Lou told the *New York Times* afterward. She mentioned how Bela Karolyi had

Mary Lou with her parents and coach, Bela Karolyi.

improved her techniques and built her confidence, then added, "Today I gave the best performance of my life."

Bela Karolyi called Mary Lou's victory the "greatest shock" of 1983.

One thing was certain—Mary Lou Retton would never be a benchwarmer again.

5 ★☆☆

"INCREDIBLE"

An American woman had never won an individual Olympic medal in gymnastics. But by the early months of 1984, Mary Lou, thanks to the steady improvement she had shown, began to look like she might be the first.

Mary Lou wowed spectators at the American Classic in California and at the American Cup competition in New York, which she won for the second consecutive year, scoring 39.50 out of a possible 40 points. Laura Cutina of Romania took second, and Julianne McNamara third.

Karolyi said that Mary Lou's performance in the American Cup was the best of her life. In her floor exercise, she started with a double back flip in a layout position. Karolyi noted that in 1976, when Nadia Comaneci was the best in the world, she never even attempted a double back flip in a layout position in competition.

Mary Lou's second move was a double back flip with a twist. Upon landing, she did a "punch front," or a standing front flip.

Commenting on these moves, a spokesman for the U.S. Gymnastics Federation said: "She lands on her back flip and then immediately, without taking a step, does a front flip. Frankly, most girls are still at the stage where they close their eyes and hope they land on their feet." He called Mary Lou "incredible."

During the early months of 1984, Mary Lou lost one friend but gained another. Dianne Durham decided to leave Bela Karolyi to live and train in Fort Worth, Texas, under Steve Krause. The move was a surprise to most people. Changing coaches in an Olympic year was not considered wise.

Some people said that Dianne was unhappy because she felt that Mary Lou was getting more attention from Karolyi than she was, and Karolyi himself said that "apparently . . . she couldn't handle the competition from Mary Lou."

While Karolyi was disappointed at the loss of Dianne, he was cheered by the fact that her place was to be taken by 18-year-old Julianne McNamara of San Ramon, California. Mary Lou remembered Julianne from the Caesar's Palace Invitational the year before, the American Cup meets in New York, and other competitions.

Julianne had been living and training under Don Peters in Huntington Beach, California. Kathy Johnson, 24, another Olympic hopeful trained with her. "I needed a change," Julianne said in explaining why she was switching to Karolyi. "I guess you can get stale in any environment."

Early in June 1984, Mary Lou, Julianne McNamara, Kathy Johnson, Dianne Durham, Tracee Talavera, and all the other leading American gymnasts gathered in Jacksonville, Florida, for the most important competitions of their young lives—the Olympic trials. The meet would help to decide which six women would make up the United States team.

Mary Lou looked forward to the competition. She was quietly confident of the outcome. And she did not disappoint the hundreds of fans who journeyed to Jacksonville to watch her compete. She finished first.

Here is a rundown of the final standings:

Mary Lou Retton, Fairmont, W. Va.	77.164
Julianne McNamara, San Ramon, Calif.	76.796
Michelle Dusserre, Garden Grove, Calif.	76.424
Pam Bileck, San Jose, Calif.	75.988
Lucy Wener, Memphis, Tenn.	75.740
Tracee Talavera, Walnut Creek, Calif.	75.516
Marie Roethlisberger, St. Louis Park, Minn.	75.500
Kathy Johnson, Huntington Beach, Calif.	75.480

Winners in Olympic trials pose with their awards. They are (left to right): Michelle Dusserre, Pam Bileck, Julianne McNamara, and Mary Lou Retton.

The top four finishers were guaranteed a place on the team. The other two would be selected from the remaining four.

The women's coaching staff, headed by Don Peters, planned to use the results of a dual match against the Canadian Olympic team in July as the basis of selection. The two women of the remaining four who did the best in that meet would be added to the team. The other two would be alternates.

A major disappointment in the trials was what happened to Dianne Durham, who had returned to Bela Karolyi a few weeks before the trials began. Dianne got off to a good start in the competition. Her scores seemed good enough to assure her a berth on the team.

But in the vault she suffered a severe ankle sprain on a landing. Doctors estimated it would take four to six weeks before the ankle was fully functional again. That meant that Dianne would miss the Olympics. She sat on a folding chair, her left leg propped, and her face in her hands as the eight qualifying gymnasts filed into the coliseum for a final curtain call.

Mary Lou's standout performance at the Olympic trials wasn't the only evidence as to how far she had progressed. An incident that took place during the trials demonstrated that as her skills had been improving her celebrity status had also been building.

Vidal Sassoon, the noted hairdresser, had been named the official haircutter for the gymnastics team. During one phase of the men's competition, Mary Lou sat in a chair in a corridor of the arena for her first Olympic coif.

As Sassoon snipped, a photographer snapped, and a cluster of Mary Lou's fans, most of whom were younger than she, looked on, oohing and aahing. When Sassoon had finished and Mary Lou had left, the girls scrambled for the locks of Mary Lou's hair left on the floor.

"She drove herself with the determination of a tiger."

As the Olympics drew near, Mary Lou was ready. She had been thoroughly toughened, both mentally and physically. Perhaps nothing demonstrated that toughness better than an incident that occurred about six weeks before the Games began.

Mary Lou was at a gymnastics camp in Louisville, Kentucky, with Bela Karolyi, when her right knee suddenly locked. She could not move her lower leg.

Mary Lou broke down and cried, really cried. "Oh, my God," she thought. "It's all over for me."

Doctors examined her and found that a piece of cartilage had broken loose inside the knee and wedged itself in the knee joint. It could be compared to taking a rolled up magazine and jamming it between the hinges of a door. You cannot move the door. For the same reason Mary Lou could not move her leg.

When she called her mother, she was on the brink of hysteria. "Something terrible has happened," she sobbed.

Mary Lou's parents immediately launched a search for a specialist to treat her condition. Dr. Richard Gaspari, director of the Center of Excellence Program at St. Luke's Hospital in Richmond, Virginia, was the one they decided on. Mary Lou was flown to Richmond where she met her parents.

A tiny scope was inserted into the knee to enable Dr. Gaspari to view the damaged cartilage. Surgery to remove the cartilage was performed through the scope.

The next day Mary Lou was walking. The day after she was jogging. The day after that, she was back in the gym, working on the parallel bars.

In the days that followed, she worked and worked to bring herself to peak. "She drove herself," Karolyi later said, "with the determination of a tiger."

Two weeks before the Olympics opened, the gymnastics teams of the United States and Canada competed in a special pre-Olympic meet. Mary Lou earned 79.80 points out of a possible 80.00 during the competition.

There was no way Mary Lou was going to miss the Olympics. No way she was going to lose.

6 ★☆☆

THE GAMES BEGIN

The 23rd Summer Olympic Games, scheduled to open in Los Angeles on July 28, 1984, was to be one of the greatest sports spectaculars of all time.

Week by week excitement built. News of the Olympic trials in gymnastics, basketball, swimming and diving, and track and field dominated the sports pages through much of June and into July. Tickets for the events, which were scheduled at such venues as the Los Angeles Coliseum and Pauley Pavilion on the campus of U.C.L.A., were snapped up fast.

The ABC television network was calling it "the biggest show in the history of television." A worldwide audience of 2½ billion was expected to watch.

American athletes were looking forward to the games with extra enthusiasm, grateful for the chance to participate. In 1980, when the Summer Olympics were held in Moscow, Americans did not take part. President Jimmy Carter had ordered a boycott of the 1980 Games to protest the Soviet invasion of Afghanistan, which had taken place late in 1979. Canada, Japan, China, West

Germany, and more than fifty other nations had joined the United States in refusing to participate in Moscow.

It was hoped that the 1984 Games would have a truly international flavor. But those hopes were dashed early in May when the Soviet Union stunned the world by announcing it was pulling out of the 1984 Games. Why? Many people said it was simply a reflection of the poor relations between the United States and the Soviets at the time. Bulgaria, East Germany, Cuba, Czechoslovakia, Poland, Hungary, and several other nations within the Soviet sphere joined the boycott.

Women's gymnastics was hit hard. The boycott meant that Russia's Natalia Yurtchenko, the world all-around champion, would not be competing. Nor would Olga Mostepanova, another member of the Soviet team and the world balance beam titlist, or Boriana Stoyanova of Bulgaria, the world champion in the vault.

Also absent would be Maxi Gnauck of East Germany. To some, Gnauck was the world's best performer on the uneven bars. She won the gold medal in bars competition in the 1980 Olympics.

But the Romanian gymnasts would be coming, and Romania always had a powerful team. After all, Romania was the country that Nadia Comaneci had represented. In 1984, the Romanian squad featured Ecaterina Szabo, a 17-year-old with plenty of seasoning in international competition.

Mary Lou and her teammates arrived in Los Angeles early in July to make final preparations. Along with hundreds of other American athletes, they stayed at the Olympic Village on the campus of the University of Southern California.

Security was very tight. Uniformed guards seemed to be everywhere. Helicopters were often overhead. Mary Lou could not leave or enter the Olympic Village without showing proper credentials. She was not permitted to receive telephone calls. Her room in Webb Tower, in fact, had no phone.

Like the other participants, Mary Lou received two admission tickets for family members, which she gave to her mother and father. But Shari and Mary Lou's three brothers would have to be content to watch on television.

Whatever disappointment anyone may have felt about the absence of the Soviets and their friends vanished with the opening ceremonies in the Los Angeles Coliseum and the kindling of the Olympic flame.

Kettledrums boomed and trumpets blared. There were chimes and cannons.

Big copper and white balloons were released. Skywriters painted the Olympic rings against a blue sky. A 750-piece marching band formed an outline of the continental United States on the field.

In the style of a Hollywood extravaganza, eighty-four pianos appeared between the columns at one end of the stadium, and the pianists played *Rhapsody in Blue.* There was an unforgettable "card trick" which involved the entire Coliseum crowd of 93,000. The spectators were instructed to hold up cards which were beneath their seats, and in so doing they created the flags representing each of the nations participating in the games.

And then the athletes from 140 nations marched around the 4½ acre Coliseum infield. When the 573-member U.S. team marched in, the huge crowd stood and cheered. Thousands of spectators waved small American flags.

The athletes took assigned positions in the infield and the Olympic flag was brought in. A one-thousand voice choir sang the Olympic hymn. By this time dusk had fallen.

Finally the Olympic torch was carried into the stadium and handed to Rafer Johnson, the 1960 Olympic decathlon champion. He climbed to the top of the stairs at one end of the Coliseum, turned and saluted the spectators with the torch, then ignited a fuse above his head that carried fire to the main torch.

It all worked to spiritually lift the athletes, to inspire them. Great performances were expected.

In the weeks before the Olympics, Mary Lou often lay in her bed with her eyes closed and let her imagination romp. She would visualize herself on each piece of equipment, performing her best routines and hitting every move perfectly. She imagined what the tension would be like, the roar of the crowd and the feelings she might have when standing on the podium, hearing "The Star Spangled Banner," watching the flag being hoisted and being presented with a medal.

The American male gymnasts undoubtedly had dreams too, and theirs were the first to be realized.

On the night of July 31, the U.S. men's team beat the favored world champion Chinese team, 591.40 to 590.80, in the men's finals. Five out of the six American men were in the ten top scorers among the eighty-one competitors. It was the first American victory in men's gymnastics in fifty-two years, or since 1932, when the Olympics were also held in Los Angeles. In the individual apparatus finals, American men took two golds, a silver and three bronzes.

Meanwhile, the women's team competition was getting underway. The beam was first.

Pam Bileck of the United States team, whose weakest event was the beam, gave a better-than-hoped-for performance, earning a score of 9.6.

Then things began to go wrong for the Americans. After one flip, Michelle Dussere had to grab the bottom of the beam to keep from falling off. She received a dismal 9.4.

Mary Lou often found herself missing home and family, but the realization of her dream made it all worthwhile.

Tracee Talavera, who followed Michelle, fell to her knees during her dismount, and was punished with a 9.15.

Poor performances weren't the Americans' only worry. Don Peters, the U.S. team's coach, lodged four protests over the marks given his charges by Romanian judge Julia Roterescu. Time after time, Roterescu handed the Americans scores that were four- and five-tenths of a point below those given by the other three judges.

But whenever she judged a Romanian, she was over-generous. For example, Roterescu gave one Romanian girl a 9.90 despite a near fall. The rules state that when a performer comes close to falling there is to be an automatic .2 of a point deduction.

One hassle over the scoring occurred just before Julianne McNamara's turn on the beam. The judges argued for several minutes. During the long wait, Julianne paced nervously.

When her turn finally came, she lost her balance on a backward flip and tumbled to the mat. Her teammates gasped. Julianne had to settle for a 9.2.

"It was a freak thing," she said afterward. "It never happened before."

With the Americans having so much trouble, the Romanians jumped out into a 1.75 point lead, and seemed unbeatable. Coach Don Peters gathered the American team about him. "It's not over yet," he told them. But most observers knew that it was.

The Americans whittled away at the Romanian's lead. Julianne McNamara put on a spectacular performance on the uneven bars, her lean and muscled legs slicing through the air like knife blades. When she swung into her handstand on the top bar, Julianne held it for just the right amount of time, and gave an elegant, slightly-arched line to her body. At other times, she moved so fast on the bars she looked as if she might go soaring off into space.

"Right now," said Bela Karolyi, "Julianne is the best bar performer in the world."

McNamara's brilliance was confirmed when she received a perfect 10 for her performance. In the floor exercise, she scored another 10.

Like Julianne, Mary Lou tried valiantly to bring the American team back after their disastrous showing on the beam. On her vault, she earned a 10 by bounding onto the apparatus, pushing high into the air, and twisting 360 degrees while doing a double somersault.

But the 10s earned by Retton and McNamara, which were the first ever by Americans in Olympic competition, were not enough to close the gap. The Romanians won the team title by 1 point: 392.20 to 391.20. China took the bronze medal with 388.60.

The silver medal won by the American team represented the first women's team medal the U.S. had won since 1948. But the medal didn't impress Mary Lou. She was downcast after the team competition. She had hoped that she and her teammates would be able to do what the men had done and win a gold. She couldn't be satisfied with anything less.

Mary Lou looked ahead eagerly to the next day when the all-around competition would begin. The leading performers from each country would compete on all four pieces of equipment. The all-around was the most coveted of all gymnastics prizes, and Mary Lou was determined to win it.

7 ⭐✩✩

FLYING HIGH

Each woman's score in the team events carried over into the all-around competition. Mary Lou had the lead with 39.525 points.

But trailing Mary Lou by only .15 of a point was the superstar of the Romanian team, Ecaterina Szabo. Tied for third place were Julianne McNamara and Romania's Laura Cutina. Both had 39.200.

Seventeen-year-old Szabo had much more experience in international competition than Mary Lou. She had won the European junior championships in 1980 and 1982. While she now ranked as Romania's national champion, she had finished third behind two Soviet women in the 1983 world meet, but now, with the Soviets absent, no gymnast in the Olympics had better credentials than Szabo.

Ecaterina had been a pupil of Karolyi's in Romania at the age of five. He once charged that Romanian officials had advanced her age by two years—when she was 13, she was suddenly pushed ahead to 15—so that she could compete in senior events, and thus benefit from stronger competition.

"Well, at least she's about my size," Mary Lou said of her rival. "You know, we're both about 4 feet 9. I've seen her work and she's terrific."

Then Mary Lou added with a grin, "But what she doesn't know about me is that I'm tougher than she is."

The crowd of about 9,000 stood and cheered when the performers marched into the arena. Mary Lou, Julianne McNamara and Kathy Johnson, the three Americans competing in the all-around, wore stunning American-flag leotards that flaunted red and white stripes down one arm and over the chest, and white stars against a blue background across their bottoms.

Off to one side and behind a barricade, Mary Lou spotted Bela Karolyi in the photographers' pit. Hardly a photographer, Karolyi was there unofficially, having obtained a pass as an equipment adjuster.

Everytime Karolyi yelled at her, Mary Lou would nod at him and punch both fists into the air.

Retton and Szabo were in separate groups for each event. In the rotation schedule, Szabo always performed before Retton. This meant that spectators, both in the stands and at home, could easily compare the scores of the two.

Beginning on the beam, Szabo dazzled the crowd—and the judges. She not only executed risky stunts flawlessly but also gave her entire routine the appearance of a magnificent ballet performance.

At one point she unleashed four consecutive backward handsprings. No other top ranked gymnast would even attempt more than two. When Szabo came soaring off the beam with a double back somersault dismount, the crowd went wild. The judges rewarded her performance with a 10.

Retton, on the uneven bars, was somewhat less than perfect. The judges handed her a 9.85 for her unsteady routine.

Suddenly Retton's .15 lead had been erased. The two women were now deadlocked at 49.475.

Karolyi, shouting words of encouragement from behind the barricade, was not worried. He realized that many competitors would have given up at this point. "But not Mary Lou," he said afterward. "Very few have her power to keep going like a bulldozer to get what they want, to go on and win."

Things went from bad to worse for Mary Lou. In the floor exercise, Ecaterina demonstrated outstanding control of her 4-foot 9-inch, 89-pound body. What's more, the Romanian did part of her routine to "The Battle Hymn of the Republic," a song as American as basketball or hot dogs. Ecaterina seemed to be flaunting her enormous talent. Her routine drew a 9.95.

While Ecaterina was occupied with the floor exercise, Mary Lou moved to the beam, mounting with a stag leap and daring backward tuck somersault. But, with two shaky landings during her routine which the judges duly noted, she got a 9.80.

When the score flashed on the board, a great wave of boos went up from the crowd. They thought she deserved better. Karolyi was livid and his face turned the color of the bright red stripes in Mary Lou's uniform.

Now the score was:

Szabo	59.325
Retton	59.175

Mary Lou's opportunity of winning a gold medal seemed to be drifting away. More than a few observers thought at this stage that she would have to console herself with a silver and even that was no certainty. Two talented Romanians, Laura Cutina and Simona Pauca, were beginning to challenge her.

But Mary Lou was still confident. She had the floor exercise and the vault coming up—her two strongest events. Mary Lou, far from surrendering, was getting ready to attack.

And attack she did. In the floor exercise she began with a sensational double back somersault in the layout position, and wore a dazzling smile on her landing. She followed with three different kinds of double backs and finished with a twisting somersault.

A routine that strong had to be worth a 10, and that's just what Mary Lou got.

Meanwhile, Ecaterina, on her vault, was guilty of a slightly shaky landing, scoring 9.90. The Romanian's lead had been cut to .05 of a point.

Szabo	69.225
Retton	69.175

The stage was set for a showdown. Up first on the uneven bars, Szabo spun like a trapeze artist. Mary Lou glanced at her and could see she was doing well. But when she was awarded a 9.90, Mary Lou knew that the door had been left open a crack. What she had to do was turn in a perfect vault.

If she were to get a 10 on her vault, the final score would read:

Szabo	79.125
Retton	79.175

Mary Lou would be the all-around titlist by .05 of a point. If she scored 9.95, she and Szabo would be tied for the gold medal; anything less than a 9.95 and she would have to be content with a silver medal.

Mary Lou went over to the barricade where Karolyi was standing. Even before he could give her any last minute advice, she said, "I'm going to stick it!" meaning she was going to stick to the mat when she landed, land without the slightest trace of wobble.

"Stick, stick, stick," she kept thinking to herself as she

went back to take her position at the end of the runway. The green light over the scoreboard flashed on. Mary Lou raised her right arm to the crowd, then bounded down the runway, rocketed off the springboard to fly some 14 feet. In the air, she combined a back somersault with a double twist, her body stretched out flat like a knife blade.

And then she stuck it, landing upright and rock still. She stood there for a split second as the crowd's cheers washed over her, then she jumped up and down, her fist clenched over her head.

Karolyi vaulted over the barricade to give her a bear hug. "Princess! Princess!" he screamed. Then he lifted her into the air and Mary Lou tossed back her head and laughed and laughed.

Don Peters suddenly appeared to chase Karolyi away. The Romanian coach was not permitted on the floor, and Peters was afraid that Karolyi might cause Mary Lou to be disqualified.

While all of this was going on, the crowd was chanting, "10! . . . 10! . . . 10!"

Karolyi believed that Mary Lou had earned a 10. Mary Lou *knew* she had. Finally it flashed on the scoreboard for all to see: "10."

Mary Lou, wanting to share her moment of triumph with the crowd, hopped back on the runway to wave and shake her fists in triumph as millions watched on television around the world.

But Mary Lou had to interrupt the celebrating to comply with a rule that stated that each gymnast must do two vaults, with the higher score being the one that counts. Since Mary Lou got a 10 on her first vault, a second one would have no meaning. Nevertheless, a rule is a rule, and Mary Lou got ready to vault again.

Her second vault was a carbon copy of her first, and she got another 10. "I stuck that one, too," she later said.

Mary Lou's winning vault. Her back somersault with a double twist . . .

and making it "stick."

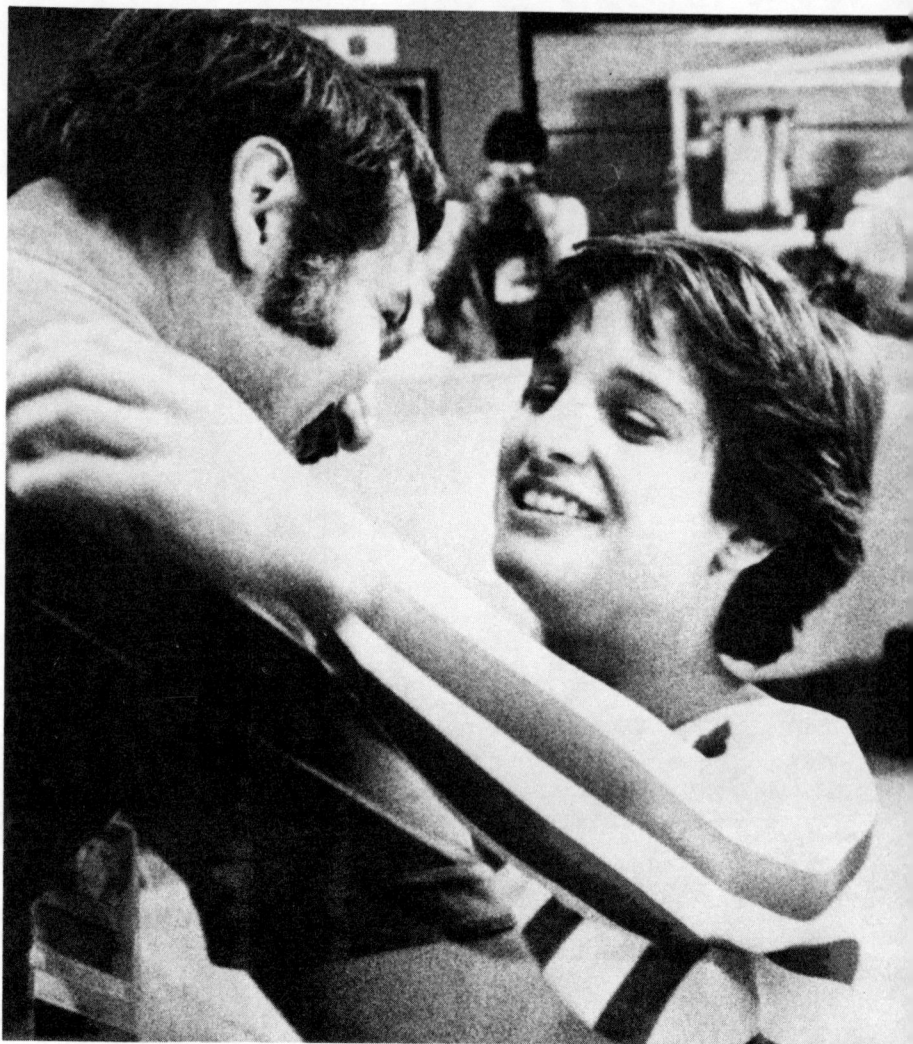

In a moment of sheer joy, Mary Lou and coach, Bela Karolyi exchange a warm hug.

Afterwards as she stood on the podium, the gold medal draped about her neck, listening to "The Star Spangled Banner," she put her hand over her heart, cocked her head, and smiled.

"I was too happy to cry!"

8 ★☆☆

POSTSCRIPT

The Olympic gymnastics competition was not over. Far from it. Mary Lou had captured the big prize, the all-around title, with her "vault without a fault," as *Sports Illustrated* called it. And the Romanians had won the team competition. But still to be decided were the individual titles on each piece of apparatus.

This competition was limited to the eight best performers in each event, who were chosen on the basis of scores they had compiled during the team competition. No country was permitted to have more than two performers in any one event.

In the 1968 Olympic Games, Linda Methany had won recognition by finishing fourth in the balance beam competition, and thus became the first American woman ever to qualify for the individual apparatus finals. None had since—until Mary Lou and her teammates arrived upon the scene in 1984.

Mary Lou herself qualified for the finals in all four events, becoming the only woman from *any* country *ever* to do so. Julianne McNamara was eligible for competition in floor exercise and on the uneven bars, while Kathy Johnson qualified on the balance beam. Tracee Talavera was to compete in the vault.

The individual apparatus finals thus presented an opportunity for each gymnast to win a gold medal in her specialty or, if not a gold, perhaps a silver or bronze. But while the competition opened with great promise, it ended on a sour note, at least for Mary Lou.

Julianne McNamara and Ecaterina Szabo were the stars of the individual apparatus finals. Not only did Julianne score a 10 and share a gold medal with Ma Yanhonig of China on the uneven bars, but she also scored a 10 and won the silver medal in floor exercise.

Julianne had been the first to compete in the floor exercise. When she had finished her routine, just before Ecaterina was given the green light, a power failure blacked out Pauley Pavilion for about seven minutes. When power was restored, Julianne's 10 flashed on the scoreboard. Then Ecaterina, in an outstanding pressure performance, went out and matched Julianne's 10. Because she had a higher preliminary score, the gold went to Szabo.

As for Mary Lou, it was generally agreed that her floor exercise performance was superior to that of Ecaterina. She got higher in the air; she did more difficult routines. But she stepped off the mat briefly on one of her landings. She was marked down to a 9.85 as a result, and thus ended with a bronze medal.

Ecaterina Szabo also won a gold medal in the balance beam competition. Her routine was almost perfect, earning her a 9.95. In the preliminary round, she had scored a 9.85, giving her a total of 19.80.

But her total was matched by that of her 14-year-old teammate, Simona Pauca, who had a 9.90 in the finals, and two gold medals were awarded to Romanian women.

The bronze medal in beam competition went to Kathy Johnson. From Huntington Beach, California, 24-year-old Kathy described herself as the "graceful old lady" of the American team. She won the bronze with just such a graceful performance.

Controversy marred the competition in the vault event, during which each contestant had to perform two different types of vaults. On her first vault, a front one-and-one-half in a pike position, that is, with her body in the shape of a *V*, Mary Lou got a score of only 9.80. On her second, a layout full Tsukahara, she earned a 10.

But Mary Lou was edged out by Ecaterina Szabo and had to be satisfied with a silver medal.

Mary Lou did not take her defeat graciously. Afterward, she and Bela Karolyi complained that Szabo had broken the rules by not performing two different vaults. They said that both of the Romanian gymnast's vaults were Cuervos.

Mike Jacki, executive director of the U.S. Gymnastics Federation, didn't agree with Mary Lou and her coach. He explained that Szabo had listed two vaults with the judges, one a Cuervo and the other a Tsukahara, both of which involve a twist in the takeoff. The difference in the twist portions of the Cuervo and the Tsukahara was a matter of timing. Jacki said "It's up to the judges to decide whether she performed it as a full-twisting Tsukahara or a sort of an early-twisting Cuervo. The judges obviously felt it was acceptable."

But that did not end it. The next day at a press conference Mary Lou continued to protest. "I don't want to sound conceited or cocky, but I was shocked," Mary Lou declared. "I felt my vault was a lot more superior. I went higher and farther.

"In the finals, you're supposed to do two different vaults. She did not."

The judges disagreed, of course. And American team coach Don Peters would not back her up.

Most observers agreed that this was not one of Mary

Lou's finest moments. Fortunately it was forgotten in the excitement of the post-Olympic celebrating.

And there was, after all, much to celebrate. Mary Lou's performance in the Games went beyond her wildest dreams. She had won five medals:

- A gold medal in the all-around competition.
- Two silvers, one as member of the second-place American team, and the other on the vault.
- Two bronzes, one in floor exercise and the other on the uneven bars.

But these were merely the tangible souvenirs. The best was yet to come.

WOMEN'S GYMNASTICS
1984 MEDAL WINNERS

All-Around
Mary Lou Retton, U.S.A. (Gold)
Ecaterina Szabo, Romania (Silver)
Simona Pauca, Romania (Bronze)

Floor Exercises
Ecaterina Szabo, Romania (Gold)
Julianne McNamara, U.S.A. (Silver)
Mary Lou Retton, U.S.A. (Bronze)

Balance Beam
Simona Pauca, Romania, and
Ecaterina Szabo, Romania (tie for Gold)
Kathy Johnson, U.S.A. (Bronze)

Vault
Ecaterina Szabo, Romania (Gold)
Mary Lou Retton, U.S.A. (Silver)
Lavinia Agache, Romania (Bronze)

Uneven Parallel Bars
Ma Yanhonig, China, and
Julianne McNamara, U.S.A. (tie for Gold)
Mary Lou Retton, U.S.A. (Bronze)

Team
Romania (Gold)
U.S.A. (Silver)
China (Bronze)

9 ★☆☆

MARY LOU MANIA

Although the gymnastics competition had ended, the Olympic Games were far from over. Another full week of competition was scheduled in such events as boxing, diving, volleyball, wrestling, and track and field.

Instead of being a spectator that week, Mary Lou decided to return home to Fairmont for a few days, then go back to Los Angeles for the closing ceremonies of the Games. She had not been home for ten months, since the previous October, when she was recovering from a wrist injury.

It would be nice to see her parents, her sister Shari, and her brothers. Besides, there was little to do at the Olympic Village. She wasn't going to be able to attend the remaining events and security precautions were such that her activities were limited in the Village itself.

Mary Lou had no idea of how much excitement she had stirred up in Fairmont. On the night she had won the gold medal, the town's fire trucks and police cars had raced through the streets with their sirens screeching.

Her fans were in a frenzy. They stole the mailbox from in front of her parents' home and hacked out clumps of grass from the front lawn.

From the moment her plane landed at Clarksburg's Benedum Airport, about twenty miles south of Fairmont, until she finally reached home several hours later, Mary Lou was caught up in a spontaneous outpouring of love and joy unlike anything she had ever experienced before.

Several radio stations in the area announced the time for her arrival and thousands of fans rushed to the airport.

When her plane landed and Mary Lou, wearing a bright yellow dress, stepped out, the big crowd cheered and waved American flags and gold ribbons. A huge gold and white banner declared: Go for the Gold, Mary Lou.

She kissed and hugged her parents, Shari, and her three brothers. Her grandparents, Joseph and Carmella Retton, were there too, and Mary Lou showered them with affection.

Still another kiss went to Jay Rockefeller, the governor of West Virginia (and also a candidate for the U.S. Senate), who arrived by helicopter. The governor told her she was "the greatest thing ever to happen to the state of West Virginia."

After ducking into the airport terminal to be with her parents and relatives for a few moments, Mary Lou emerged to wave to the crowd again. Police tried to keep the throng behind a yellow rope, but the screaming fans surged forward to surround Mary Lou. People were pushed and shoved in every direction. Two children went down in the melee, one of them into a huge puddle.

A news conference had been planned, but the crush was so great it became impossible. Someone provided Mary Lou with a chair to stand on.

She waved and flashed the smile that had by now become famous. "I'm shocked," she said, looking out at

The parade honoring Olympic winners in New York City was only one of many which lined the streets across America.

the throng. "I can't believe it. To have all of this support is great," she added. "It feels so good to be back home."

Asked what she planned to do that night, she grinned and said, "Sleep—wonderful sleep."

A white convertible awaited Mary Lou. It was meant to whisk her from the airport to Fairmont where a parade had been planned. But Mary Lou's well-wishers caused an enormous traffic jam that delayed her departure for more than an hour. Eventually the cars got sorted out, and the convertible with Mary Lou in it sped north on the interstate toward Fairmont, heading a motorcade that stretched for almost two miles.

A crowd had begun to gather in front of the Marion County Courthouse in the center of Fairmont late in the afternoon in anticipation of Mary Lou's arrival. They numbered in the thousands by the time Mary Lou arrived in darkness on the outskirts of town, where she boarded a Fairmont fire engine decorated with red, white and blue crepe paper. Police cars and the fire truck led the procession which snaked its way through city streets.

Quickly-made banners and signs had gone up all over town. Several said: We Love You, Mary Lou, and Fairmont's Golden Girl. Precious Gifts Come in Small Packages another declared. Gold ribbons hung from lampposts and flagpoles.

The crowds cheered and waved signs when their star passed by. "Mary Lou! Mary Lou!" they chanted. Many spectators spilled out onto the street in excitement. Some passed bouquets to her. Hundreds photographed her.

The motorcade stopped on Merchant Street to listen to a musical salute offered by the East Fairmont High School Band. Someone handed a bullhorn to Mary Lou, who was now wearing her five medals, so she could address the crowd.

Mary Lou is whisked off in a white convertible after landing at airport on her return home.

"I'm overwhelmed," she said. "I can't believe the support Fairmont has given me. All I can say is that it's great to be home."

Everyone in Fairmont remembers Mary Lou's homecoming. "It was something that Fairmont and Marion County had never seen the likes of," said the *Times–West Virginian*, "and may not again."

Later in the month, a Mary Lou Retton Day was proclaimed in Fairmont. It was highlighted by an "official" homecoming parade. Despite fierce thunderstorms that evening, thousands of area residents turned out to welcome Mary Lou at Fairmont's East-West Stadium.

Mary Lou was in demand everywhere. She appeared on "The Johnny Carson Show" with guest host Joan Rivers. She chatted with Rivers about the years spent preparing for the Olympics and how her life had changed since winning. But what seemed to excite her most was talking about her new 1984 Corvette that boasted "Mary Lou" plates and was "fully loaded."

West Virginia Governor Jay Rockefeller invited Mary Lou to the state capital in Charleston. Also to be honored was Ed Etzel. From Morgantown, West Virginia, Etzel had won an Olympic gold medal in small-bore rifle competition. The governor proclaimed a "Mary Lou Retton and Ed Etzel Day."

During this period, something else happened that was probably just as exciting to Mary Lou as all the applause and cheers, the receptions and parades. Accompanied by two of her brothers, Mary Lou appeared one morning at the Fairmont office of the West Virginia State Police to take the test for her driver's license—and she passed.

What more could a 16-year-old girl with an Olympic gold medal and a red 1984 Corvette ask for?

The events in Fairmont gave Mary Lou a foretaste of what was to come. Over the next few weeks, she and the

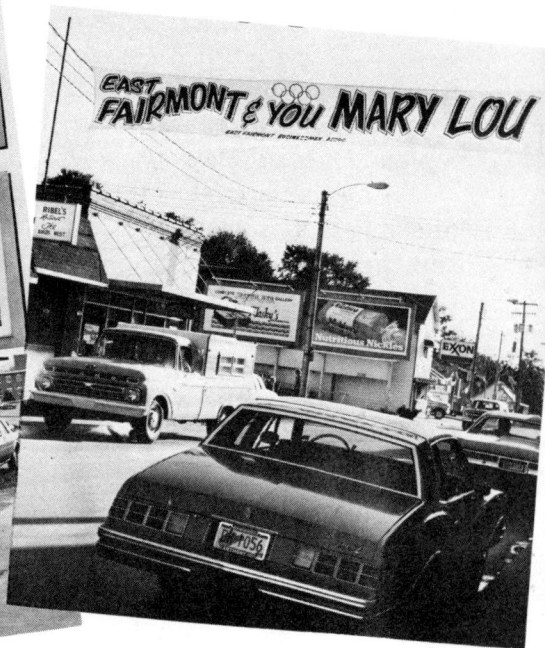

other medal winners were the focus of joyous celebrating from one end of America to the other.

The Southland Corporation (which owns and operates 7-11 stores) sponsored a five-day tour for the more than two hundred Olympic medalists. It began with a breakfast at a hotel ballroom in Los Angeles where Mary Lou, basketball star Cheryl Miller, and swimmer Steve Lundquist were designated to make the President and Mrs. Reagan honorary members of the 1984 Olympic team. It was Mary Lou's responsibility to put a bright red team blazer on the President's shoulders.

At first it seemed like an impossible task because of the difference in their heights. "Can she reach you?" asked President Reagan's wife, Nancy, as Mary Lou stood on her tiptoes and held the blazer high for the photographers' cameras. The President averted a crisis by bending his knees. After putting on the jacket the President reached down and hugged Mary Lou.

Following the breakfast, the President delivered a short speech. In it he praised the medalists and thanked their coaches, trainers, parents and friends. "You're heroes," he said. "Everyone of you is living proof of what happens when America sets its sights high and says, 'Let's create a little excellence.' "

Washington, D.C., New York City, Orlando, Florida (for a trip to Disney World), and Dallas were the tour cities the athletes were to visit. They traveled in a pair of chartered airplanes which were met by a fleet of buses intended to whisk the athletes away to whatever events had been planned in their honor.

The visit to New York City was one of the tour's highlights. There, a ticker tape parade had been planned, where the athletes would march up New York's "Canyon of Heroes" for ceremonies in their honor at City Hall.

Mary Lou's proud Fairmont neighbors posted signs all over town to show their appreciation.

No one was prepared for the tremendous outpouring of people who came to pay tribute to the athletes. They packed the sidewalks from curbside to the building lines along the route of the march, and spilled into the side streets for blocks. New York's Mayor Ed Koch said that more than two million people were there, while the *New York Times* called it the largest parade anyone could remember.

A blizzard of paper—ticker tape, ribbons, confetti, computer punch cards, and scraps of computer printouts—cascaded down upon the athletes. At times the downfall was so intense it blotted out the sun and blue sky.

Mary Lou, wearing a white-and-red striped top and a white skirt, marched with the first group of medalists. Sometimes she walked with the Mayor, while other times she and Julianne McNamara walked side by side.

The crowd roared its approval as the athletes went by. Often chants rang out. "Atta way, U.S.A." was one of them. Or simply, "U.S.A. U.S.A. U.S.A.," shouted over and over.

And at times the parade watchers paid Mary Lou a special tribute, chanting, "Mary Lou! Mary Lou! Mary Lou!"

There were handprinted signs in Mary Lou's honor, too. You're the Greatest, Mary Lou, said one. Way to Go, Mary Lou, said another. We Love You, Mary Lou, a third proclaimed.

The parade route was about a mile long. Before the official ceremonies on the steps of City Hall got underway, the marchers paused at the Tweed Courthouse for iced tea and lemonade.

During the break, Mayor Koch said to a reporter, "Do you know what Mary Lou told me? This parade ain't nothin', because she already got a ride on a fire engine in her hometown."

Mary Lou talks to reporters while standing beside Mayor Edward Koch of New York City.

Putting his arm around Mary Lou's shoulder, the mayor said to a photographer who had his camera poised, "She's a real politician. She knows how to mug for the camera just like the rest of us."

What did Mary Lou think of the wild scene? She shook her head in disbelief. "It's really hard to deal with," she said. Later at City Hall, standing on a chair so she could see over the speaker's stand, she declared, "The people of New York are incredible. *I mean incredible!*"

It was an unforgettable experience, not only for Mary Lou and the other marchers, but also for anyone who witnessed the event. For one watcher, however, the memories of the day were not happy ones. Fourteen-year-old David Katz from Merrick, Long Island, came into New York by himself for the first time just to see Mary Lou.

"I was never that interested in gymnastics," he said. "Then I saw Mary Lou and it was love at first sight. I loved her floor exercise."

David waited patiently amidst the great crush of spectators for the parade to begin. Finally, he saw the police motorcycles and two flatbed trucks containing photographers that led the way. He saw the marching bands and the clusters of smiling and waving athletes.

But where was Mary Lou? The parade went by so fast that David missed her.

10 ★☆☆

RICH AND FAMOUS

In the weeks following her Olympic victory, Mary Lou's life was transformed. She could no longer step out of the house without being recognized. People were always stopping her on the street to ask for an autograph or to pose for a snapshot.

Mary Lou tried wearing sunglasses to disguise herself. But when you are 4-foot-9 and have been seen in virtually every living room in America, sunglasses are futile.

"You look like Mary Lou Retton," a fan would say.

"No, I'm Sally Smith," Mary Lou would answer with a grin. And then she'd laugh, giving herself away.

The telephone at Mary Lou's parent's home rang constantly. She estimated they were receiving about 300 calls a day. Before long, callers began hearing this announcement: "The number you have reached—363-7615—has been changed to an unpublished number."

Many people thought that Mary Lou would like to have a videotape of her famous vault, the one in which she scored the 10 that won her the all-around title. Mary Lou received forty tapes depicting the vault in the six weeks following the Olympics.

Letters by the thousands arrived at the Retton home on Beverly Road. Since a souvenir hunter had confiscated the mailbox, the letters had to be delivered at the front door.

Some letters were addressed simply, "Mary Lou Retton, Olympic champion," but she still received them. A handful of letters contained marriage proposals from men she would never meet. The Rettons stored the letters in big garbage bags until they could figure out how to answer them.

Beverly Road was officially changed to Mary Lou Retton Drive.

Two songs—"Go for the Gold" and "The Winner"—were written in Mary Lou's honor by Seseen Francis, a Fairmont songwriter. Described as "kind of Top 40 with country influence," the songs were recorded by *The Other Brothers* from West Virginia.

Mary Lou received hundreds of offers from corporations to endorse their products. Network television executives wanted her to make guest appearances.

She hired an agent, John Traetta, president of National Media Group and Highbar Productions, to sift through the offers and recommend those he thought to be the best.

Traetta was unique as an agent because he had considerable experience in gymnastics. From 1965 to 1975, he had been the head gymnastics coach at DeWitt Clinton High School in New York City, and his teams were undefeated in those ten years.

In the early days of cable television, Traetta both broadcasted and produced gymnastics events for the medium. This led him into the production of a variety of other sports events for cable television networks. He also began representing sports personalities as an agent.

Early in 1984 he worked with Mary Lou during a gymnastics meet in Chicago. He was certainly impressed

The former Beverly Road is now known as Mary Lou Retton Drive.

by her gymnastics skills, but also with her magnetic personality. After the Olympics he spoke to Mary Lou about becoming her agent, and she accepted.

Traetta put a high price tag on Mary Lou's services. According to one report, only multiyear deals at not less than $200,000 a year were to be considered, and any company signing Mary Lou would have to put money into gymnastics. Traetta told the *Washington Post*: "She is definitely going to be a leader in the sport, and her image is going to have a large effect on the growth of gymnastics."

Mary Lou had no intention of retiring as a gymnast. "I haven't reached my peak yet," she said. "There are a lot of things I still want to do."

Not long after her Olympic triumph, she resumed working with Karolyi. "I still listen to him," she said. Any deal Mary Lou signs has to leave time for her to train.

The first three contracts that Mary Lou signed were with Wheaties, McDonald's, the fast food corporation, and Vidal Sassoon, the hair styling and hair care company.

The Wheaties contract was notable because it named Mary Lou an official Wheaties spokesperson. Bob Richards, the Olympic gold medalist in the pole vault in 1952 and 1956, and Bruce Jenner, the 1976 decathlon gold-medal winner, had previously represented Wheaties as spokespersons. Mary Lou was the first woman to do so. She was also pictured on Wheaties cereal boxes and appeared on the company's television commercials.

The first Wheaties commercial featuring Mary Lou didn't even mention her by name. It didn't have to. Mary Lou's image was instantly identifiable to television watchers.

Mary Lou's contract with McDonald's called for her to be a worldwide spokesperson for the company's youth sports program.

After she signed her contract with Vidal Sassoon, Mary Lou got a new " 'do." "It's lighter now—highlighted," she said, "and is supposed to go behind the ears."

Mary Lou was also expected to endorse a line of sports apparel and a soft drink. Of course she would be doing guest spots on television shows.

Mary Lou's new life could be compared to a game of Pac-Man. The challenge was to see how many gold dots she could devour before monsters devoured her.

Mary Lou displays both her new hairdo and her talent on the balance beam during post-Olympic tour.

The gold dots were the endorsement contracts and television appearances.

The monsters took the form of the demands upon her time from promoters, journalists and fans, and the almost complete loss of privacy she had to endure. As Connie Carpenter-Phinney, the cyclist who won a gold medal in the women's individual road race, put it: "I don't envy Carl Lewis [winner of three gold medals in track and field] or Mary Lou Retton or anyone who's so much in the public eye. You can't go out and be yourself."

In the video game, when Pac-Man is devoured by a monster, he withers and dies like a delicate flower in the hot sun. The "monsters" that grew out of the post-Olympic craziness could have left Mary Lou in the same condition.

But no one who knew her expected that to happen.

Mary Lou quickly learned to cope with the new set of challenges she faced. She enjoyed being a superstar; a media darling. And she had no trouble just being herself.

Mary Lou will survive. Her pretty face and winning smile, her charm, her cheerful, upbeat matter will be there for us to see for years to come.

ABOUT THE AUTHOR

George Sullivan, a notable author of books for children and young adults, has had close to forty titles published. Many of Mr. Sullivan's books focus on sports and sports figures, including one on Nadia Comaneci, who Mary Lou Retton greatly admired.

Mr. Sullivan is a resident of New York City and a member of P.E.N., The Authors Guild and The American Society of Journalists & Authors.